Christopher Whybrow was born in London in 1955 into a family of thirteen as the eighth child. His father was an electrician and his mother was a busy, very busy, housewife. The author became a telephone technician and worked for British Telecom for 15 years. At the age of 31, he moved to Austria with his Austrian wife and two-year-old son, Robert, doing various jobs. One being a language trainer while he learnt the German language. He worked then mainly on construction sites abroad and in Austria.

After injuring a shoulder at the age of 54 he was refined to being at home for a longer period of time where he, in the peace and quiet of the day, had time to play with his thoughts (over God and the world). Eventually, he put his thoughts down on paper, to create his first book, *My Soul's Human Experience*, for us to enjoy here.

My Soul's Human Experience

Christopher Whybrow

AUSTIN MACAULEY PUBLISHERS™
LONDON • CAMBRIDGE • NEW YORK • SHARJAH

A CIP catalogue record for this title is available from the British Library.

ISBN 9781398493254 (Paperback)
ISBN 9781398493261 (Hardback)
ISBN 9781398493278 (ePub e-book)

www.austinmacauley.com

First Published 2023
Austin Macauley Publishers Ltd®
1 Canada Square
Canary Wharf
London
E14 5AA

I would like to dedicate the book to my very busy and loving mother (an angel, here on Earth) and my father for his different approach and curious mind. Also, to my close family, my wife, Maria, for her great support and children, Robert, Steven and Selina for putting up with the Dad, a visionaire whose thoughts and fantasies run wild sometimes.

I would like to acknowledge here my appreciation for creating this book for my best-ever fans, who always believed my poems should be published. That would be my dearest wife, Maria, thank you. Also my good friends, Franz and Roswitha, many thanks. Also, many thanks to our creative artist, Lea Hirschl, for the cover design and the illustrations throughout the book.

Table of Content

Thoughts

Silent thoughts,
pure, clean, unhurt and clear.
Loving thoughts that leave you never lonely.
I cannot find the words or sounds,
or vibrations for the air,
to say what lays upon my heart.
My thoughts, coming from my heart,
stay locked within my mind.
Undamaged, untangled, unspoilt and untrammelled.

Are there words that can say it?
Can words say it like it really is?
Pureness and cleanliness
is in your heart and in your soul,
to be transported to your mind and to your thoughts.
The brain, our translator, our dictionary, our resolver,
is not without fault, so our words can never be,
as pure and as clean, as our thoughts that lay within.

Words translated by our thoughts are often
manipulated, twisted, confused or misguided,
by lives distracted from cleanliness and purity,
by lives hardened and formed.

Our brains, our words too quick to judge,
to criticise and to condemn.
Not wanting to know what we don't understand,

although our hearts reach out for love and harmony,
for compassion and understanding.

Let our hearts speak out for us,
before our brain translates our thoughts.

Do not be sucked into the negatives that surround our lives,
created by thought.
Don't sink, don't stay in the sump.
Look for higher ground around you.
For silence is the language of spirit,
All other is a poor translation.
Raise your consciousness and join the web of life.
The web of life that connects us to
everything there ever was and ever will be.

The Great Awakening

Is knowing that we have to face our fears.
For decades, centuries and millenniums,
we have obeyed tyranny.
Why, because they told us so,
got inside our heads, our minds.
Told us we were sinners, not divine.
Being kept in fear, until this very day.

A fear that lays so deep inside us all.
Carried with us through previous lives,
for thousands of years.
That innocent helpless, hurting child within our minds
has kept us in obedience,
Obeying all commands, all rulers and all priests,
Up till this very day.
Teachers, parents, police, wardens, authorities.
We are programmed to follow orders. Ask
NO questions!
We had no strength, no will to stand up to it,
to say NO! NO more.
'Cause we did not know, that child we carry
deep inside our subconscious
Was hurting all the time.
That hurt child, now living in an adult body.
That hurt child suppressed and never dealt with,
never healed
year after year.

Now we know, we must now grow,
Grow up become the adult being that we are.
In order to cuddle, nurse and assure that child in
ALL of us.
In order to stand up to authority, to tyranny, to evil.
Protect, show LOVE and never fear again.
Take that hurt child in your arms, hold it tightly,
go into the world,
With your head held high as the protector, as the
warrior that is no child NO more!

Freeing that inner hurt child in all of us
Is breaking the chains of slavery.
Unite in FREEDOM and leave all fears behind.
The Great Awakening.

The Human Tsunami

Soul brothers, soul sisters here on Mother Earth.
We know why we are here.
To talk and to defend our biological physical bodies.
We will unite our human family, as one.
And wave after wave, they will come.

Like a small quake on the seabed, a ripple will appear.
And the waves surfacing will be small and few.
Multiplying along the way 'til it meets the shore.
There it stands ten metres high,
the tsunami can't be stopped.

Like, a dam built to stop the water on its way to the sea.
The cracks will appear and the water
will trickle through.
Growing in length and size, the cracks will not,
cannot hold the water back,
til one day, the dam will burst and the water will be freed.
Freed to find its way, its destiny, the ocean.

Mankind's evolution can also not be stopped.
The human tsunami.
For many a year, we have lived in a daze, lived in fear.
We did not know it; we did not realise it; it just was.
Now with the Pandora's box open,
for all evil doings to be seen.
The veil is uncovered and the evil is shocking.

We must share the shock in order to end the shocks.

Now open our hearts, leave mindset behind,
and put trust in heart space.
Look the evil in the eye and hold closely to LOVE.
To gratitude, to kindness, care and serve,
be humble, be loving.
Free ourselves from the pain of separation,
from duality and competition.
Unite as one "Human Family"
and feel the comfort and safety in unity.
Let no one stand in our way 'til we reach our destiny,
Our wholeness, our oneness.

An Evolution in Motion

Over centuries, they have killed our prophets,
Called them sorcerers.
They have killed all living angels here on earth,
Called them witches.
We were then the few, they were then the many.
We are now the many and they are just a few.
We are seeing now behind the curtain,
Unveiling their lies, corruptions and evils.

We will not be stopped; we cannot be stopped.
One wave after another, one generation after another,
Waking up from our slumber, uniting as one,
One human family, of all generations, colours and
religions, releasing our chains.
Listening to the Ohm, to the call of Mother Earth.
Raising her consciousness, the Schumann resonance,
taking us with her.
Taking us into a higher realm, into a new dimension.

She sent us into Lockdown, in order to do our
shadow work.
To look inside ourselves and change our inner worlds.
To find and to see who we really are, just LOVE.
And now we are ready,
ready to break those chains around us,
And come together as one;
the once created are now the creators.

Of the world we want to see,
in harmony and gratitude of Mother Earth

The power of one human family living in unity.
We cannot be stopped.
We shall not be stopped.

Time to Awaken

Do not sit on the sidewalk too long.
Do not look away, so as not to see what's going on.
Do not close your mind and believe nothing's wrong.
Live your life positively, be happy, enjoy.
But live your life critically, ask questions! Ask why.
For the unfairness, the unjust won't leave you alone,
it will thump in your head
'til your heart starts to weep
and the cramps in your stomach, they won't go away.
If your soul is made of LOVE, unconditional LOVE.

For some and for many is the world not so bad,
but the signs are all there,
when you open your eyes, when you open your mind
Not just for pessimists but for optimists too,
it just becomes clear, when you don't turn away.

The New World Order,
Their New World Order.
Slowly taking its place, in the world that we live in.
The powers-to-be have plans for you and me.
In the dis-order they created,
through wars for regime change,
they'll want order, obedience, they will
want to control.
With the blood in their veins, as cold as ice,
they will set up a police state to keep you in line

so make sure that you nod and comply to their ways.
Now is too late, to question, to ask why!
We will fight their wars, kill one another,
while they drink champagne.

For the people's World Order
is not what they'd like,
harmony and LOVE for one another,
no profits for them.
No wars, no killings, no starving, no scarcity
and no crime,
Free energy, new technology for mankind, plenty for all.
For richness is in happiness,
in the LOVE we show and share.

Mankind will work again for the good of
Mother Earth,
for all living beings, all creatures great and small.
Everything we say and do, will thrive and shine.
In a world where we wake up,
wake up and sing with the birds.

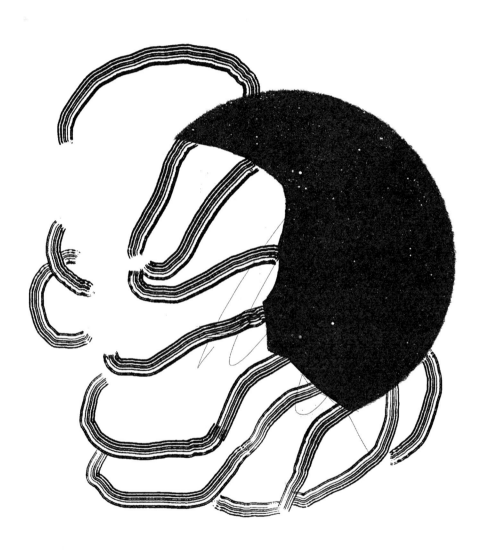

No Trust, No More

Don't know where to start,
so many things going around in my head.
Feeling like a terrorist, 'cause I question what I see.
don't believe what's being said, no more.
Don't understand the world no more.

The Twin Towers, middle of New York were sprung.
Free fall, they say, coming down in its footprint.
World Trade Centre 7
followed the same way.
Two planes, destroying three buildings.
Just don't make no sense, no more.

Evidence enough to question what was told to us.
New evidence, they do not want to see or hear,
and we should, leave it all behind.
Forget, accept, be patriotic.

The lies that they told us, took us to war.
A war against terrorists; a war with no end.
Destroying and disrupting, nation after nation.

The homes, the schools, the gardens of many.
Supporting all sides, with their money and their guns.

In occupied countries, the hate grows deep,
deep inside,

And it didn't take long to create Al-Qaeda and ISIS
So as to kill one another on the lies that were told.
Killing, killing, killing, they just want to see more.
While the money rolls in and the bodies pile high.

Now they are looking at you, looking at me,
watching what we post, listening to what we say.
To protect us from terrorists that we've never seen.
NSA, FBI, CIA will one day come for you,
not the patriot, you should be,
when you do not comply, when you do not trust.
A fascist regime wants patriots, patriots that are blind,
patriots that toe the line.

The war they created, based upon lies,
turns all that aren't blind and don't toe the line.
Into possible terrorists,
Because we will talk our mind.
So, I say to all, go seek,
go search for yourself.
The truth, the truth that is you,
Based only on LOVE,
for all living beings and all living things.

Smoky Rooms

Throughout history, plots have been laid
behind closed doors, in smoky rooms.
Control, control, control
that's all that's in their heads.
For thousands of years, one purpose, one direction,
one end.
Rule overall, no matter what it takes.
Rule overall, no matter how long it takes.

They left their homes in Babylon,
to conquer lands and divide the world.
They created fear, a fear we never knew before.
In a world full of fear, fear from each other.
They'd offer us protection with their military and armies,
but with their military and armies, they'd go to war again
and centralise their power on all corners of the globe.
To fight for peace, for a peace we all once knew,
before they went to war.

They are not protecting us,
they're protecting what's not theirs,
but man won't see it, it's too cleverly disguised.
They will cover our eyes, with problems they created.
They will open our eyes, with answers we'd believe.
Their purpose, their direction,
once only known to themselves.
Won't come quickly, they'd meet again.

In those smoky rooms behind closed doors.
They'd hand the plot to generations yet to come.
The bloodline is thick,
So thick they believe it will last forever,
the plot goes on and on.
While we, mankind, will die with peace in our hearts
and leave relations, old and young,
to start anew, the life they choose.

For the bloodlines that rule, ruled by
money and religion,
Won't match us when we all unite,
our brothers, sisters around the world,
because love is divine and that is our weapon,
that no military or army can destroy.
We will look within our souls
and change what they have done.
There will be no revolution
because what they have built will fall,
and in our evolution, we will build upon the old.
A world that's fine for us.

No use no more for smoky rooms,
so lock those doors forever.
For we now know the lessons that we learnt.
That control and rule must not exist,
where love is to be found.

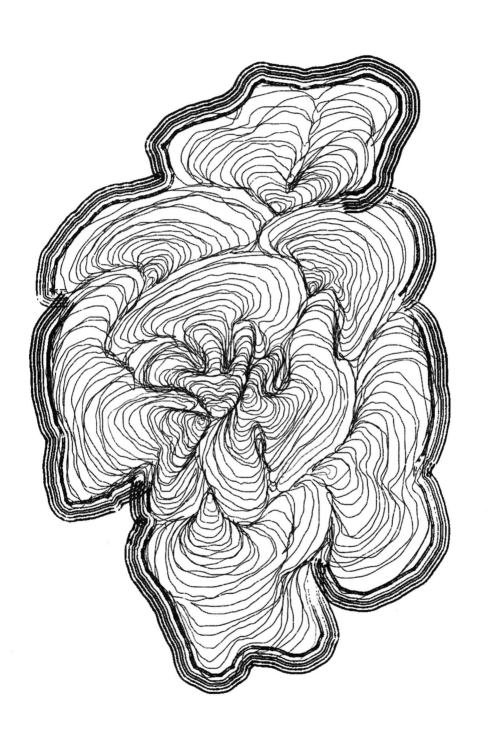

Egoist-Me

Oh why! Oh why! Oh why!
Did we listen to the powers above.
Did we listen to the powers to be.
To the powers that rule us, with their guns and
their money.

They fed us with beliefs, different beliefs.
They conquered and drew up borders, to
keep us apart.
Languages were learnt, so as not to understand all.
Politics created.
From communism to socialism, nationalism to capitalism.
Not one of these isms were ever good for us.

For the powers above, for the powers to be,
it works for their needs, it works for their wants,
but for us, just divides us and keeps us apart.

To be apart is to be alone,
to be alone is to be afraid.
So I build up walls around me and become the
egoist I am.
I am the product of the powers to be, of the powers above.
The egoist me.

We are so far apart, we don't see who's around us.
Who might need us or want us or even love us.

But when our consciousness grows
and we are aware of who we are.
You'll be there for me and I'll be there for you.

We won't need no politics, we won't need no beliefs
and the language of LOVE is the language for all.
And when we unite, together as one.
They can pack up and go, with their guns
and their money
The powers above, the powers to be.
And the ego in us, will be lost and forever gone.
In a world full of harmony, for you and for me.

Spirit, Energy, God, Consciousness

The spirit outside the body
is serene and pure and in total bliss.
In harmony – with itself,
in harmony with everything and nothing.

It feels no pain and knows no suffering.
Floating and hovering in a sea of darkness,
in the silence of our universe.
Has only pure thoughts and unconditional love
for every living being on this planet and beyond.

But the spirit inside the body
with no silence, peace or tranquillity
is confronted with a reality
that is not so innocent and fine.
Which at times can be cruel, evil and ignorant.

It will feel and see no compassion, no wholeness, no bliss.
It will witness, through the body's experience,
emotions, high and low,
and feelings of hate and happiness.
And so, the human being, mankind
has a lifetime's work to find,
what once was known outside this body's experience.

It has lessons to learn and hardships to overcome.

To find truth, bliss and happiness,
within the body that it chose.
To first find peace within itself and in its heart.
To be contented and fulfilled
with no wants or expectations
is a step towards our heaven here on earth.

Then to find in oneself a connection to all,
Because only connected,
connected with LOVE,
unconditional LOVE for all of mankind,
can the harmony on earth
be compared
with what consciousness is
outside of the body.
Only then will we have our paradise on earth.

New Start

I stood naked at the age of 31, vulnerable and lost.
I had no voice; I had no say.
I had no status.
I had immigrated to a foreign land, a foreign language.
But walked with my head up and my shoulders back.
'cause I knew, I knew I was not alone.
Angels all around me, to help me on the way.
I never was alone.

The demons tried to put me down, the angels picked
me up.
I see now that the demons were the insecure ones.
The demons were the weak; they had no self-esteem.
The demons were the jealous ones,
that did not want to understand.
The demons that thrive, thrive off others' difficulties,
trials, and weaknesses.
But I did not stand alone,
for every demon there are two angels.

Here on Mother Earth, the angels hide themselves.
In every river, every forest, mountain and lake.
And that's where I found peace;
I found understanding and clarity.
I listened to the angels, my gut feeling, my heart.
Mother Earth and the source, always by my side.
'cause when I awoke each day, the sun rose with me.

Not always to be seen, sometimes hiding behind the
clouds, but there.

I am now 65 and have found home wherever I am.
Amongst all soul brothers and soul sisters.
Of all nationalities, colours, religions and ideologies.
So, do not be afraid of a new start,
to stand naked once again.
'cause I promise you, there are more angels
Far more than there are demons.

Gap Between Heaven and Earth

Our Earth is to be found in our outer world
Whereas Heaven is to be found in our inner world,
And for thousands of years, have been oceans apart.

But the gap between Heaven and Earth
is not so far away.
Just a fine line.
Lies in our imagination, a re-think, a wish.
Felt from the heart,
'cause Heaven is just a heartbeat away.
If you turn inwards, you can sense it,
Listen to your intuition your gut feeling for clarity.
Learn to let go, let go of past habits of old,
question your beliefs.

Isolation, separation, disconnection to one another.
Manipulation of our minds, by propaganda and lies
have created our world, 'cause we only obeyed.
They held us in fear.

Our hearts are now knowing and we won't just obey.
Must move on from our fears and trust in our hearts
'Cause we are looking for that connection.
The LOVE that connects us.
We will hold out our hand and show LOVE
'cause LOVE has the power.
The only power that understands

The fear, the hate, the ego, just me.
And how it separates!!!

LOVE, unconditional LOVE, for all
and for everything,
will only come when we lose our fears.
Our fears of losing what we don't really want,
don't really need.
Beliefs and habits, will be overcome,
in the creation of our new outer world.
Then, only then will we have found
Heaven here on Earth.

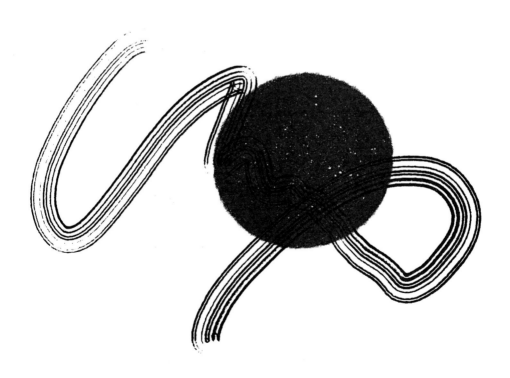

End Times, New Beginning

We are the "Human Experience"
NOT the "Human Experiment".
Under the wings of our Mother Earth, "Sophia",
we go where she goes.
We are just "bubbles of energy" of all shapes and sizes.
Light beings, consciousness, energy waves,
moving in cycles.

Those asleep now will later be awake.
Those awake now, will later have moved on.
Like they, that are first, will later be last
And the last will be first, energy cycles,
they just keep on coming.

The momentum gets stronger, gets faster
as our consciousness grows.
It is not to be stopped, cannot be stopped.
The end times are here. New times ahead.
We believed the evil, the lies
and it set us on a road of self-destruction.
A collective sub-consciousness manipulated,
so, so dark and disturbing.
She, "Mother Earth", is reigning us in, bringing
us home,
letting us remember who we are. Divine LOVE.
Revealing the lies for us to see and understand,
through our higher frequency.

The darkness has been pierced,
that imprisoned us for so long.
We are now shining our light, our LOVE into that
darkness.
We are finding our way home, to LOVE.
Returning and embracing the "Divine Source".

So, do not stay stuck in the "Rabbit Hole",
or you will not find back home.
Do not stay in the "Spirit World"
or you will not find back home.
Our job, as we are all light workers,
is to create a paradise here on earth.
We are her children; she provides and cares
for us ALL.
We are one "Human Family" in the web of life.

The Ultimate Journey

Take time to stop and to be still.
Take time not to think just for a while,
and leave the world of thought behind.
Consciousness arises when the mind is thoughtless.
Stop listening to the voices in your head.

Turn inside and make that inward journey,
to discover who you really are, to discover
your true self.
The ultimate journey to discover your divine.
To discover you are LOVE, pure LOVE,
covered by life's burdens.

Now that you are still and without thought.
Your body, your physical body
is getting heavier and heavier,
and your mind becomes lighter and lighter,
as you go in search of your soul
that lays hidden deep inside.

To find that peace, harmony, LOVE that you are
looking for,
you must first discard the many layers formed inside,
layers of desires, wants and luxuries,
the love for a plastic, materialistic paradise
That the ego thrives and feeds on.
The ego, the false self.

And the journey goes still further,
Travelling even deeper, through even more layers.
More layers to discard, to leave behind and put aside.
Layers of hate, greed, envy, mistrust and hurt.
To unravel bit by bit,
To unravel so as to let in the light.

And as you travel even deeper, your eyes see clearer,
The mind will be freed and your thoughts
will become purer,
now coming from the heart.
Your voice speaks simple words, with strong meaning
and still deeper you travel
Looking, searching for the pure LOVE that you are.
The true self.

With the true self now found,
The pure LOVE that you are and always have been
Your true found LOVE, so strong,
will soon dismantle the borders and the boundaries,
the limits of beliefs once known.
You will again connect to all mankind,
your fellow human beings.
With no thoughts or hesitations,
of colour, religion or nationality.

The Ruler and The Ruled

Those that know our story, our history,
our potential and our power.
Want to keep it from us, keep it hidden in the shadows.
While we fought battles for the bloodline,
the Imperialists, the Colonists.
Mother Earth "Sophia" we left bleeding, hurting
deep inside!

And the Gnostic teachings, that had once showed us,
once taught us.
We destroyed and annihilated.
As Victors they wrote the history books.
In order to show and exploit,
the strength they thought, they had.
The strength that we had given them.
Not knowing that the power is what WE have!

He/She who dare speak out against them,
were only few in number.
And they were quickly dealt with, to keep
our story hidden.
Tortured, murdered, terrorised,
their bodies died in mortal pain.
Their souls released.
Now the time has come, the age of technology,
the internet.
And for every prophet that they killed,

a hundred more have returned.
To take the evolution of mankind to a higher level,
Of higher consciousness, a level they don't know.
Their strength, they show in armies guns
and weapons.
Cannot match the POWER of a united Human Race.

Words are our modern-day weapon, words
from the heart.
Words used wisely until we all unite.
We will learn about our past,
cause they cannot hide the TRUTH no more.
Our knowledge will expand our POWER.
Our hearts will expand the LOVE, the love that we are.
A united "Human Race" here to create a
paradise on earth.
We will not stop 'til the last of their war toys,
end up upon the scrapyard.
We will learn to Live In Peace not wait
to Rest In Peace.

Spirit

It was formed with love,
it shall stay love.
Cells parting, multiplying, creating a wonder.
A wonder far beyond belief.
A body formed to carry and protect your soul.
Entering this world not knowing any rules, laws,
right or wrong.
For the newly formed, the newly born,
There is no name, nationality, sex or religion,
fixed within its head, fixed within its thoughts.
It is a newly born spirit,
waiting to progress, waiting to learn.
A new start, a new beginning, a new chance.
To find a world, create a paradise, here on
Mother Earth.
It is our spirit's work to reach its destiny, help it
find its way.

Like the water on the mountaintop,
seeping through the rocks, finding its way to the sea,
to its destiny.
It won't be stopped 'til it reaches the oceans so blue.
The spirit, a new born life, looking to connect to all,
Won't be stopped 'til it connects to all mankind,
to the one consciousness.

Unfortunately, the spirit gets distracted on its journey,

By the programmed sub-conscious
and lies hidden, hidden deep inside the body
built for it,
covered, hidden, imprisoned by the ego.
The ego that has a name, has a religion, a sex, a colour.
The ego, me, mine, I am, that controls the mind,
if let be.
So, return to your base form,
Let go of the ego, 'cause you are LOVE.
Be in control of the mind,
the mind that was and is, LOVE. Unconditional LOVE.
Help it find its destiny, this paradise on earth.
Let the spirit live in you.
Don't let the ego blind you
and lead you from your path.

Mankind, the Manipulated Being

For hundreds of years, maybe thousands,
Man has lived with his Subconscious mind,
in his manipulated, programmed, biological computer.
Programmed from birth, at school, in society, in
church and by his political beliefs.
TV, the media and marketing,
only believing what he is being told.
He buys things, gadgets
and identifies himself with possessions.
The ego, the false self, that's not his true face.

He is destroying his own home and he doesn't
give a damn,
'cause he's got enough money, he can buy, buy and buy.
In a state of confusion, in a state of destructiveness,
governed and motivated by the ego,
he will go to war for the want of more.
Caused by his greed, lust for power, or just
through his fear,
His ego has separated him from the all
and now he stands alone.
What he does not know or understand, he will fear.
What he fears, he will kill.

Due to belief systems and ideology
for Queen, King or Country.
Mankind has committed and accepted

slavery, torture, murder and unrest,
at home and around the globe.
His intelligence used unwisely is no more
than stupidity.

Many a philosopher gone by, many a prophet alike,
have described man's condition,
man's UNCONSCIOUS condition,
As dysfunctional, mad, or a mental disorder
because natural disasters haven't killed as many people
as mankind has each other in their wars,
revolutions and ethnic cleanings.
It is programmed as the norm, to allow the wars,
that give him more.
He doesn't see, just looks away,
accepts the wars all around him, it is the norm.

So, empty your mind, rid yourself of those thoughts;
it is time to awaken; it is the time of awareness,
now is the moment.
Forget the past and tomorrow will come all on its own,
in due time.
Be aware of the moment, the CONSCIOUS mind.
Question what you do not understand,
Stop what you do not like.
Know yourself and not the borders of your beliefs.
You are a human being and not a human doing.
Listen, see, smell and feel the life that has
always been there,
but your thoughts were of yesterday or maybe tomorrow.

Be in control of your thoughts and stay present.
Do not wander off with the clouds.
The present moment is beautiful, peaceful,
calm and real
and your thoughts in the now will become
your new reality.
Your new world.
For you are the truth, go be what you want,
go do what you feel from your heart.
If all that you do is on the basis of LOVE.

Now with your ego diminished and your soul set free,
your CONSCIOUS mind is your newfound life,
our COLLECTIVE CONSCIOUSNESS,
our new found world.
Then, only then, can this paradise on earth be enjoyed
by all.
So, reprogram your biological computer,
with data from the heart,
that is only the presence.

The Magic of the Rabbit Hole

The magic of the Rabbit Hole.
Make you mad, make you sad.
Keep you learning what it's all about
And leave you only more in doubt.
Don't let it drag you in, 'til you can't get out.

The magic of the Rabbit Hole,
Will keep you popping in and out.
To make you shout what you just found out.
Hearing the problems, what's going on, what's
going wrong.

The magic of the Rabbit Hole,
Will lock you in, not let you out,
If you do not realise, there are no answers there to find.
The answers lie outside the hole.
'cause when you've seen enough,
you'll look inside your soul
To find the answers, find solutions,
that were not in the Rabbit Hole.
To what's going on, what's going wrong.

Connecting to the real world,
to Mother Earth and all she has.
Connecting to your soul brothers, to your soul sisters,
to mankind.

Time to come together as one
And face the fiend, the mutual fiend, that's waging war
on "humanity".

We are one "human race" with the universe
as our parents.
Your DNA a micro version of the source, a
universe within.
You are unique, you are divine, you are the power.
That will find the answers, find the solutions.
That were not to be found down in the "rabbit hole".

Information Overload

Our hearts feel it, our hearts know it
That something drastically is wrong, but not sure what.
Not right to look away, so as not to see.
Will only give me sleepless nights. Hear noises
in my head.
Information overload.

What shall we talk about?
Climate change, 5G, geo-engineering, trans-
humanisation.
Can't make it out, can't work it out;
something doesn't seem right.
Head is spinning, stomach cramped, while my
heart weeps.
Information overload.

What shall we talk about?
Covid 19, vaccines, masks, anti-social
distancing, refugees.
Confused, turning around in circles.
Can't laugh no more, no quality time no more.
Information overload.

What shall we talk about?
The animal Holocaust, terrorism, child trafficking,
Big pharma.
Doubting the media, confused, no trust no more.

Back down the "rabbit hole" I go.
Information overload.

My physical outer world, running wild,
running out of control.
Can't change it, can't influence the outcome, out there
Won't look away, no more. Must end my ways,
must change the journey that I am on.
Look inside myself, look into my inner world.
Must find calm, must be at peace within.
Find gratitude, find LOVE, unconditional LOVE.
Contentment.
Must keep outside the "rabbit hole"
and shine my light now where I know.
In order to raise my consciousness,
in order to find the New Earth!

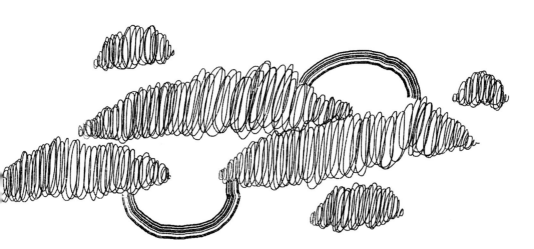

Who Is the Enemy?

We faced up to the enemy. We faced up to the beast.
We fought wars and we won.
Caesar, Stalin, Hitler, Mao Tse Tung, Napoleon, all fell.
We came, we saw, we conquered.

One war after another and nothing ever changed,
'cause we did not really know the enemy,
'cause we never did know the beast.
We fought to draw up borders.
So as to call a country "mine" and keep all others out.
We fought, we killed, we tortured
And thought it was all right.

We saw nothing, we were blind.
So, the lessons were repeated, time after time.
We never could see, so we never could learn.
That the enemy, the beast,
lies deep within the programmed mind.
And so we never could move on
and evolve to a higher consciousness.

The enemy, the beast, is in the mirror to be seen.
With every selfish thought, with every "Ego", wish
or want.
With every hurt that's being done
With every lie, we tell or spread.

To look away and ignore the evil being done.
To deceive and cheat our fellow man.
'Cause until we learn to change within, to LOVE,
to help,
To be as one,
Our collective thoughts will find another enemy,
another beast.
To keep us all at war.
Separate, isolated, divided and alone.

Eyes of Fear

Eyes of fear and helplessness,
are eyes of those who think alone.
Who stands alone, not knowing they are one with all.
Lost in a world of loneliness and stress.
With eyes wide open, that cannot see beyond the hurt.

Now close your eyes and look inside your heart.
Open it up and never be alone again,
in a world that doesn't care.
Closed eyes unfold the stress that's on your mind.
Heals your pains and soothes your worries.
Eyes closed, to look for peace that's there to find.

You've looked inside your heart,
now open up your eyes and let your heart see for you.
Open up you heart and let your woes be told.
Share your fears with others.
Lessen them with every word that's spoken.
Open up your heart and never be alone.

Talk and share your worries, don't hold them
closed within.
Say it as it is, for ears of empathy to hear.
There is no right, there is no wrong,
only lessons to be learnt on or journey through this life.

Don't let your mind control your heart.
The mind becomes hardened, while the heart
remains pure.
The heart is there to show the way,
follow it, trust it. It will never let you down.

The eyes that were once full of fear.
Let them see thru your heart,
so as not to be alone,
or ever on your own.
For eyes that see from the heart,
are eyes that see no lies.

Love Yourself First

Get to know yourself,
Everything about you.
Become one with yourself
Learn about your body,
it's the one that you have chosen.
Be aware of what you have,
for it is the home of your soul.

Feel your lungs expand,
as you breathe the air around you.
Imagine the blood
running in your veins like a river.
Hear your heart beat,
as it pumps life through your body
and the thoughts in your head,
pay attention, 'til they're cleaned.

Feel your skin, feel your bones, feel your muscles,
A functioning system, wrapped in a parcel,
Your body, a mobile apparatus, the transport
for your soul.
Enjoy the life, the energy, that exists within your skin.
Look after it, look after it well, for it is the
universe within.
Then at the end of the day, let it unwind,
Let it slow down, relax and rest,
to return to its base, its stillness, its darkness.

To centralise itself and prepare for the morning.

Only when I am one with my body
and one with my thoughts,
can I connect, connect with the world, the
world outside,
and expand my found oneness, the love for myself,
extend my love further, further afield,
to my partner, my children, to my family of all forms.

But the journey's just started,
I have a world that's to love.
A world to be learnt, to be discovered, to be loved
and now I can start cause my roots are secure,
my roots have dug deep,
for I found love and a closeness to my body
and my soul.
Now I'll look further for the love of mankind,
for the love of all beings in my home on Mother Earth.

A Cuddle

Our eyes meet, no words needed.
One step forward and our cheeks touch.
You feel my breath upon your neck.
I run my fingers thru your hair
Your heart misses a beat
as you search for air, a breath to snatch.

The heart now beating faster.
As I wrap my arms around you.
Your body feels weak and your head empty.
You could just let go, become weightless.
But you don`t.
So I squeeze you a little tighter
and as you feel my strong arms gripped around you
you sink into my chest and sigh.
Burying your face, closing your eyes
The moment is yours as you just let go.
Your knees start to tremble, you feel you are floating.
No worries, no fears, no thoughts.
You just feel safe.

It was only a minute but it seemed like forever.
As I set you down and steady you.
Your heart now opened wide.
You feel happy and you smile at me contented.

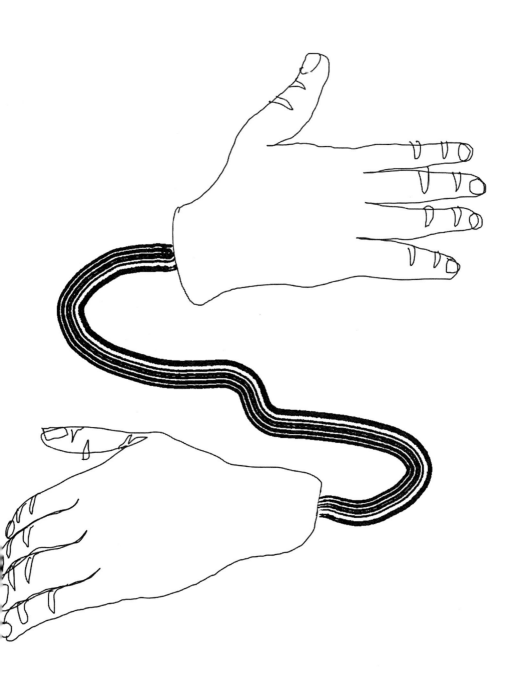

True Love

The true LOVE you are dreaming of,
longing for
Is first to be found within,
Within you, within your inner world.
'cause only from there can it manifest.
Live, listen and feel into the heart space
What your soul is looking for,
Understand your soul.

LOVE yourself,
LOVE what you do,
What you do untold, unspoken for others.
Be the ears that listen, the hand that offers hope.
Be the shoulder for someone in need of comfort.
Be humble, have a smile for all that can want it.
Share unconditional LOVE around the world.
Have time.

Be true to yourself take time for yourself.
Send out that message of LOVE into the outer world.
The universe will listen,

The universe will reward you.
When and however it can, be patient, be LOVE.

Then true LOVE will find you.
It is that simple, just trust,
'Cause LOVE is all there is. That is the bottom line.

Falling in Love

She came into this life one day, as she walked by,
Two people, two spirits,
not knowing they were meant to meet.
It started with a glance, a look into each other's eyes,
and neither knew what was to come.
An attraction so powerful, a connection so strong,
like two magnets, never to be pulled apart.

The heart pumping harder, the blood running faster.
A feeling in the stomach, he never knew before.
One nice word, a telephone number,
that's all that it would take,
for these two souls to find one another,
to combine and become complete.

A date, so late in the evening to exchange thoughts.
To listen, listen and learn about each other,
to laugh and just enjoy the moment,
and when their hands make contact,
or their arms and legs brush by on another
Reminds them of the love they've found.
That feeling in the stomach, once again,
and from that moment on, the time that's spent alone
is like living in a room of empty space.

Laying close together with their legs entwined,
their genitals resting close on one another.
While their hearts beat as one.
Cheek on cheek so soft and warm,

with lips so close, just waiting, waiting for the taste.

Their arms wrapped around each other, in the parcel
of love.
Waiting to be unwrapped, waiting to explore more.
This feeling deep inside the stomach,
waiting to break free and shoot right up the spine,
to explode and be released, released inside their heads.

Croatia

Looking out over the lagoon, at the deep blue waters.
The warm gentle night air is upon us.
As the sun says goodbye to the moon.
Setting in the West, the sky is on fire.
It is dusk, it is dark as the moon rises to the occasion.
Reflecting its powerful pastel light on the water.
It blows kisses on the water
and it responds with ripples.

I feel connected as a breeze comes over me.
Mother Earth whispering in my ear, taking a breath.
I feel her pulse along with mine.
Her heart is full of joy. I sense it and it makes
me smile.
A living organism, like you and like me.
The ultimate mother of all living beings,
we bless her.

The stillness belongs to the darkness.
The calm, the peace to the night.
I close my eyes, I AM.
I AM the darkness, the calm, the peace, the night.

The lagoon lies still
As we let go of the day gone by
And allow our dreams to manifest.
Who knows where we go when the lights go out?

Only to awaken, to the sun rising in the East.
A warmth, a light, that stirs us gently from our dream.
The dawn here once again, saying good morning.

The River

Gathered rain upon the mountains,
seeping through the rocks,
Waiting to emerge,
Waiting to find a way, to surface and be free.
Once surfaced, there is no stopping it.

The damp mountain rocks,
soon to form a brook, soon to form a stream.
A stream that's gaining volume, gathering momentum,
from high above, it falls, falls, falls.
Water falling with such a strength and beauty
to the eye.
Smashing against the rocks and spraying far and wide,
Whatever's in its way, whatever it can reach
waiting to lay still a while,
in the lake it formed, below the falls,
before it starts again, its long, long journey to the sea.

This brook, this stream, is now a river,
increasing in size as it flows.
Ripples forming, as the winds gust upon it,
small, tiny ripples dancing, shining in the sunlight.
Soothing and calming, whoever cares to share.
This journey to the sea.

'Til it hits the bend and turns to rapids,
racing faster, not letting any stock or stone stop it on

its way,
cutting out the mud along its rugged banks.
It won't be stopped, it can't be stopped,
'til it sees its destiny.

You can try to stop it, build your dams,
but the land will perish,
and people's homes will be washed away.
So don't deny the river, its destiny, its journey
to the sea.

Oh, let man take a lesson from the river running free,
and not be denied the road that takes him to
his destiny.
He must emerge and find a way to surface and be free.
He must stay critical and honest to himself and
to mankind,
to seek what he is looking for.
And let no one build dams from debt,
to stop him in his tracks.

For they that do, will perish
on the land where they once lived
and the walls of Babylon will crumble once again.

The Spring

The days are longer and the nights are getting shorter,
as the sun rises higher, higher than before.
Its warmth and energy becoming stronger day by day
As the winter leaves us once again.
and the spring creeps in.

Snow melting on the mountain peaks,
filling the rivers with its cold, crystal clear waters,
trickling, pouring, uncontrolled, over stock and stone,
on its newly started journey to the sea.

Deep below the soil, an energy awakening,
in the roots of every plant and tree.
Ready to move through its veins once again,
and explode into blossom.
The animals once sleeping and in hiding,
covered to keep warm, with stomachs getting hungry,
Start to stir and waken and open up their eyes.
Knowing that the fruits are ready and waiting there
for them.

Man is also shedding his jacket,
woolly hat and winter shoes,
leaving them behind, on the hanger in his room.
He blossoms in his bright coloured jumpers,
and light trousers.

Letting him and others know that spring is in the air.
Once again.

The sun, the source, our life, our power.
Shining through our window on a sunny day
in spring.
Telling us to stand up, stand up and not to miss
The evolution that's in motion,
that comes with every spring.
So, kick off your blanket and throw up your arms.
Take a deep breath
and enjoy the new birth, of a new day
That comes with every spring.

We Are All Just Actors

In this lucid vibrational body, that houses my soul,
For its short time here, here on Mother Earth.
I'll have the chance, as a Human Being.
To live out a story, my story.
Have the leading role, be the star in my film.

I choose the experiences that I make.
I choose if I'm the victim or the warrior,
the hero or the fiend.
In my human experience,
I will witness all emotions to be had.
I am an actor on the stage, looking for a happy end.

And when I go to sleep at night,
I will awaken to who I really am.
I'll switch off the film, just for a while.
Release myself from the physical world, open the
third eye.
The eye that awakens with the darkness
and closes when it's light.

I will leave my body and return home,
Where all and everything is one.
To play, talk and laugh in thought, in heart space.
With my soul sisters, with my soul brothers.
Experiences shared in thought will be my dream.

The dream, I bring back with me,
When I open my eyes and switch on the film
that's playing.

When I die, the actor dies and my film is to an end.
The character forever lost.
My body stops and all energy returns to the source,
within my roots.
To power up my soul, my true self.
Filling up my chakras full.
Reaching up and out through my crown.
The kundalini is achieved and my soul is set free.
Freed from its physical existence.
Releasing me, my soul, my true self, known as LOVE.
Into the atmosphere above, I melt into one with all.

Our Visitors from Afar

They came from the heavens above,
on a journey through the galaxies.
To find a planet, to find a star to make their home.
Leaving behind a lifeless mass, a destroyed existence.
Caused by their want of power and greed for more,
to rule by the sword.

The fallen angels, the guards of the sun.
So called by the Sumerians from times gone by.
Looking to start afresh, looking to rule again,
on their newly found home on Mother Earth.

They mingled with mankind
and the women bore their offspring.
Nephilim, the giant ones, a bloodline meant to rule.
They landed in the Middle East and Africa,
then spread afield, this so-called privileged being,
to the North, the West and to the East around
the globe,
keeping the bloodline blue, as blue as it is true.
The fallen angels, with their reptilian brain,
interacting in a parallel world.

Their knowledge and technology
far beyond that of mankind.
They created a money system, to keep them in control,

give you anything you want, as much as you want,
then change the rules, the rates, the percentages.
To keep you locked inside, the prison without bars.

They will have you now relying on the resources
they supply
They won't allow a new technology
to be found and used for free.
Control is all they want,
at the cost of all mankind and the nature we all know.
All for money, all for profit, to keep them in control.

The fallen angels, the guards of the sun,
the giant ones, the Nephilim,
will one day leave our Mother Earth, our home,
a lifeless mass, a destroyed existence,
if man stays in the darkness, with his blindness.

Mankind's Re-Birth

In these testing trying moments of uncertainty,
Confronted with so many options, possibilities
and choices.
First negatives then positives, to be felt inside our gut.
The pendulum is swinging to and fro like crazy.
Cannot settle, cannot relax,
worry and concern coming from the heart.

The re-birth of humanity is here upon us,
it has begun; there is NO going back.
We have left the comforts of our mother's womb
(Sophia)
And have entered the birth canal
of mystery and the unknown.

It is not easy in this present moment, can see no light.
Everything is getting tighter, getting narrower.
Our fears, we are forced to put aside.
'cause we must push, there is no choice.
Pushing our way into the unknown,
into the mystery that awaits us.
This turmoil that we feel inside us,
emotions, feelings running wild

is the uncovering, unveiling of our own doubts
and distractions within us.

We are sorting it, preparing ourselves
for we do not know what.

At the moment, there is NO light to see.
But like in any birth, it will appear.
Cause there is no going back, we want to be free.
Soon to smile, smile and open our eyes slowly,
cause the light is too bright.
Welcome to the new earth, our new earth
called paradise.